W9-ASY-629

PTEROSAURS

A TRUE BOOK®

by

Elaine Landau

Children's Press®

A Division of Scholastic Inc.

New York Toronto London Auckland Sydney
Mexico City New Delhi Hong Kong
Danbury, Connecticut

A pterosaur fossil

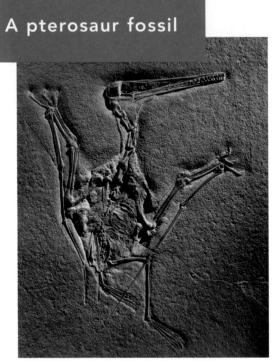

Content Consultant
Susan H. Gray, MS, Zoology,
Little Rock, Arkansas

Reading Consultant
Cecilia Minden-Cupp, PhD
*Former Director, Language and
Literacy Program
Harvard Graduate School of
Education*

Author's Dedication
For Klara

*The illustration on the cover
and title page shows a
pterosaur in flight.*

Library of Congress Cataloging-in-Publication Data
Landau, Elaine.
     Pterosaurs / by Elaine Landau.
          p. cm. — (A true book)
     Includes bibliographical references and index.
     ISBN-10: 0-531-16829-8 (lib. bdg.)   0-531-15470-X (pbk.)
     ISBN-13: 978-0-531-16829-5 (lib. bdg.)   978-0-531-15470-0 (pbk.)
     1. Pterosauria—Juvenile literature. I. Title. II. Series.
QE862.P7L36 2007
567.918—dc22

                                                                                              2006004427

CHILDREN'S PRESS, and A TRUE BOOK™, and associated logos are
trademarks and/or registered trademarks of Scholastic Library Publishing.
SCHOLASTIC and associated logos are trademarks and/or registered
trademarks of Scholastic Inc.
3 4 5 6 7 8 9 10 R 16 15 14 13 12 11 10 09

Contents

Flying reptiles called pterosaurs filled prehistoric skies.

What's That in the Air?

Imagine traveling millions of years back in time—before there were people on Earth. If you looked up at the sky you would not see birds or airplanes. They did not exist yet either. Instead you might see flying reptiles soaring through the air. Back then the world was filled with different kinds of **reptiles**.

Dinosaurs—reptiles that lived on land—roamed Earth. Huge reptiles that looked like sea serpents swam in the waters. Flying reptiles called pterosaurs glided

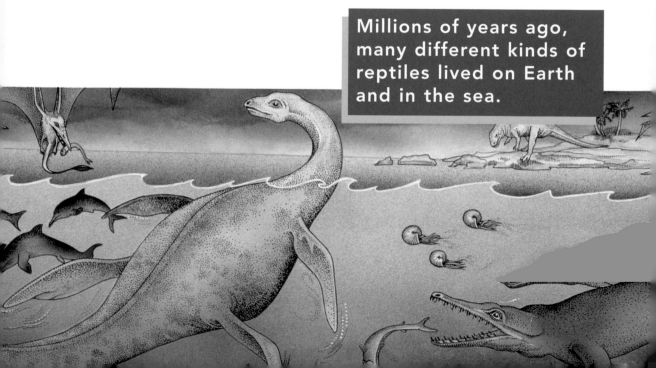

Millions of years ago, many different kinds of reptiles lived on Earth and in the sea.

These pterosaurs are catching
dragonflies for dinner.

through the air. They lived during
the Age of the Dinosaurs. The
Age of the Dinosaurs was 250
million to 65 million years ago.

Prehistoric pterosaurs were an interesting group. They were neither dinosaurs nor birds. They were flying reptiles. There is nothing like them alive today. If you want to know more about these unusual creatures, just read on.

Introducing Pterosaurs

What did a prehistoric flier look like? It is hard to say. Flying reptiles were different sizes. Some smaller reptiles had a wingspan of about 12 inches (30 centimeters). Wingspan is the distance from the tip of one wing to the tip of the other wing.

In this fossil, you can easily see the long wings and narrow head of this pterosaur.

The largest pterosaurs had wingspans of about 40 feet (12 meters). They looked like small airplanes in flight.

The earliest pterosaurs had long tails, while the later pterosaurs had short tails. They also had long wings and necks, and many had long, narrow heads. In some cases, their heads were as long as or longer than the rest of their bodies. Their long heads helped to keep them stable

The heads of some pterosaurs were almost as long as their bodies.

in flight. Their large skulls balanced their bodies.

Many pterosaurs also had a large, bony **crest**, a comb or a feathery tuft, on the top of their heads. Some crests were about the size of an apple. Others were quite long and pointed. These may have helped to steady these reptiles in flight. Crests also may have been useful in finding mates.

This pterosaur's bony crests are pointed.

Spotlight on a Special Pterosaur: Meet *Pteranodon*

Pteranodon had a very long neck, head, and beak.

With a wingspan of 23 feet (7 m), *Pteranodon* was among the larger pterosaurs. This toothless, winged reptile had a very long neck and **beak**. *Pteranodon* also had large wings that allowed it to glide easily through the air.

Scientists think that *Pteranodon* could have taken its **prey** from the

Pteranodon, with a roomy lower jaw for fish and a large, bony crest

ocean. It could have plucked fish from the water with its long beak and swallowed them whole. Like today's pelicans, *Pteranodon* had a roomy skin pouch beneath its lower jaw for storing fish. *Pteranodon* also had a large, bony crest growing out of the back of its head.

Pterosaur skulls show us that these animals had very large eyes. Good vision would have been important to any flying creature. These animals had to spot their prey from up high. After spotting the fish,

The large eye holes in this pterosaur fossil show how big the animal's eyes were.

Not all pterosaurs went diving for fish. This one filtered tiny plants and animals from the water.

they would have to swoop down to catch it. An animal with poor eyesight would have a hard time catching its dinner!

Perhaps the pterosaur's most interesting body part was its fingers. Three of its fingers were the same size and had claws. Its fourth finger, however, was very long. It served as the front edge of the pterosaur's wings. This fourth finger had four bones that formed the wing's frame. Pterosaur wings were covered with leathery skin.

Paleontologists are scientists who study prehistoric life.

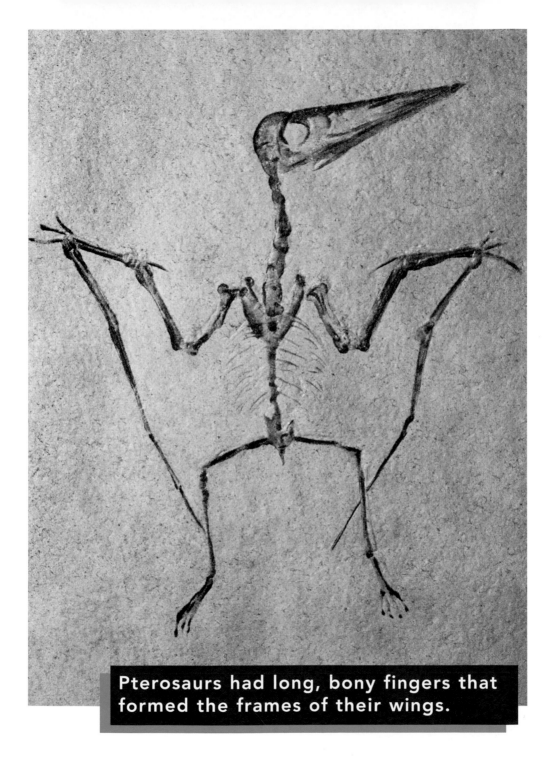

Pterosaurs had long, bony fingers that formed the frames of their wings.

These paleontologists are searching for pterosaur fossils in Brazil.

Paleontologists are not sure what color pterosaurs were. They believe that these prehistoric fliers might have been many different colors, just like today's reptiles. It's likely that males and females were different colors.

Paleontologists believe that pterosaurs were many different colors.

Spotlight on a Special Pterosaur: Meet *Quetzalcoatlus*

Quetzalcoatlus was the largest flying animal that ever lived.

Quetzalcoatlus was the largest flying animal that ever lived. Its body was about 20 feet (6 m) long, and it had a wingspan of 40 feet (12 m)! Even its beak was about 6 feet (1.8 m) long. That is about the height of a tall man.

Can you imagine how big *Quetzalcoatlus* was?

Today, the whooping crane is the largest bird in the United States. *Quetzalcoatlus* was as big as five whooping cranes.

Some paleontologists think that *Quetzalcoatlus* fed on dead animals. Perhaps it spotted the dead bodies of dinosaurs or other animals from the air. After swooping down, this flying reptile would have picked at the animal flesh with its beak. Once it was full, it would take off again.

Flying *Quetzalcoatlus* were probably easy to spot from the ground.

Fossil Discoveries

Paleontologists learn about pterosaurs by studying **fossils**. Fossils are evidence of plants and animals that lived long ago. Fossils might include bones, footprints, teeth, or leaf imprints on rocks. Paleontologists find fossils and piece them together like a jigsaw

Fossils help us to learn more about pterosaurs.

puzzle. This gives paleontologists a better idea of what
prehistoric animals were like.

Few pterosaur fossils have
been found. Pterosaur bones
were hollow and lightweight.
The bones were great for

flying because there was less weight to carry. But often these lightweight bones were too fragile to last long enough to create fossils.

Fossil hunters have had some luck, though. They have found fossils from different kinds of pterosaurs in Europe, Asia, and Africa, as well as in North and South America. These fossils have led paleontologists to believe that pterosaurs may have lived in

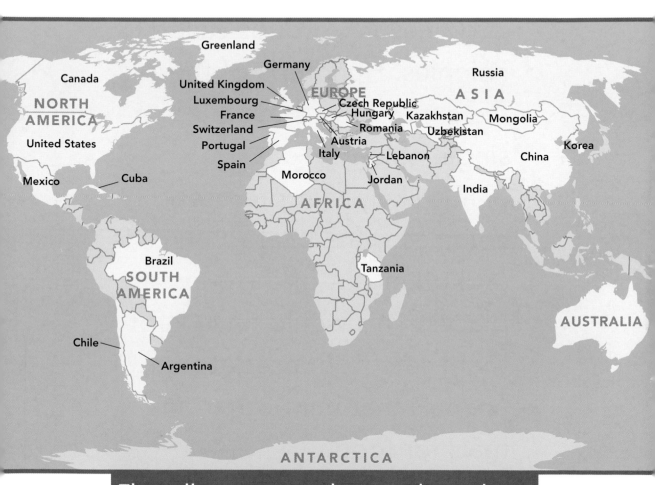

The yellow areas on the map show where pterosaur fossils have been found.

large nesting groups called colonies. Hundreds of these fliers may have stayed in a single colony.

It is likely that pterosaur colonies were located on cliffs and other out-of-the-way places. This would have kept them safe from **predators**, animals that hunt other animals for food.

Paleontologists have also studied the skull fossils of these flying reptiles. There is

All these pterosaurs are probably from the same nearby colony.

no way to know exactly how smart pterosaurs were. But the size of the **brain cavity**, or opening in the skull where an animal's brain is located, offers some hints.

Scientists often compare an animal's brain size to its body size. Animals with brains that are larger than expected for their body size are thought to be smart. So scientists think pterosaurs might have been as smart as today's birds.

Some pterosaurs plucked fish from the water the same way many present-day birds do.

Pterosaurs acted a lot like birds. Fossils show that a female pterosaur probably sat on her eggs until they hatched. Her mate probably

A small, modern-day bird brings food to its young. Pterosaurs may have fed their young the same way.

brought food back to the nest for her. Paleontologists think that newborn pterosaurs were not able to fly right away. Their parents may have fed them until they were ready to fly out of the nest. Today's birds do the same for their young.

Paleontologists have a lot of other questions about pterosaurs. What did they do when they were not flying? Did they walk on two feet like birds? Or did they crawl on all fours like bats?

These questions are hard to answer. Dinosaurs left many fossil footprints, but pterosaurs left few. These prehistoric fliers did not spend much time on the ground. They also nested on rocky cliffs, where it wasn't possible to leave footprints.

A few pterosaur tracks have been discovered, however. The most recent tracks were found in Wyoming. These tracks seem to show that pterosaurs walked on all fours. However, paleontologists haven't found enough tracks to know for sure.

Extinction

Many people think pterosaurs became extinct, or died out, at the same time as the dinosaurs. But that is only partly true.

Various kinds of ancient reptiles lived, and then became extinct, at different times during the Age of the Dinosaurs. No one knows why certain kinds of ancient reptiles died out when they did. But 65 million years ago, all the remaining pterosaurs and dinosaurs were gone.

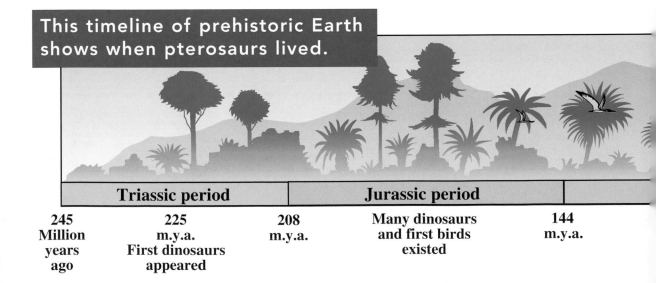

This timeline of prehistoric Earth shows when pterosaurs lived.

Triassic period		Jurassic period	
245 Million years ago	225 m.y.a. First dinosaurs appeared	208 m.y.a.	Many dinosaurs and first birds existed	144 m.y.a.

No one knows for sure why pterosaurs and dinosaurs became extinct. During the Age of the Dinosaurs, Earth was still changing. The large landmasses called continents had not finished forming.

(Note:"m.y.a." means "million years ago")

| Cretaceous period | Tertiary period | |

65
m.y.a.
Last dinosaurs
became extinct

1.6
m.y.a.
First humans
appeared

Spotlight on a Special Pterosaur: Meet *Pterodaustro*

Pterodaustro fossils have been found in South America. This pterosaur was interesting because of its jaws. This flying reptile had long, thin jaws that curved upward. Its lower jaw was packed with hundreds of long, thin teeth. There were as many as five hundred teeth on each side! The upper jaw had short teeth that combed through the lower teeth in the same way you pull a comb through your hair.

Scientists think that *Pterodaustro* was a filter feeder, eating fish and small water animals. A filter feeder such as

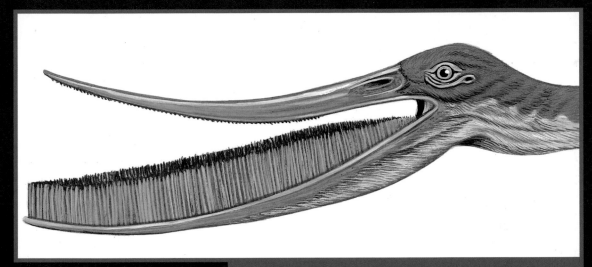

Pterodaustro's mouth contained a bristlelike filter for catching fish.

Pterodaustro skims the water with its mouth open. As the seawater flows through its jaws, its lower teeth filter, or trap, the prey. Then the food is swallowed whole.

Another way that *Pterodaustro* may have eaten was by scooping up food from the water and filtering the food through its teeth.

Seas and mountain ranges were still taking shape. Different kinds of plant life appeared. The dinosaurs and pterosaurs were likely unable to adjust to all these changes.

Many paleontologists believe pterosaurs and dinosaurs became extinct after an asteroid crashed into Earth. An asteroid is a large, planetlike body that travels through space. If an asteroid crashed into Earth, a huge

Many paleontologists think an asteroid crashed into Earth, causing pterosaurs and dinosaurs to die out.

crater, or hole, would have formed. The dust thrown up from the crater would have floated up into the **atmos-**

phere. It would have formed thick, dark clouds that blocked out the sun.

Without the sun's warmth, Earth's climate would have turned quite cold. Pterosaurs, dinosaurs, and other forms of life would not have been able to survive this climate change.

We may never know as much about pterosaurs as we would like. That is because they have no relatives in today's animal world.

Pterosaurs fly through the air just before asteroids hit the ground.

In some ways, these prehis-toric fliers may always remain a mystery of the past.

To Find Out More

Here are some additional resources to help you learn more about pterosaurs:

 **Books**

Arnold, Caroline. **Pterosaurs**. Clarion, 2004.

Foran, Jill. **Dinosaurs**. Weigl, 2004.

Harris, Nicholas. **Dinosaurs**. Blackbirch, 2002.

Matthews, Rupert. **Pterodactyl**. Heinemann, 2003.

Organizations and Online Sites

Project Exploration
950 East 61st Street
Chicago, IL 60637
http://www.info@projectex-ploration.org

This organization works to increase students' interest in paleontology.

Sternberg Museum of Natural History
http://www.oceansofkansas.com/Sternbrg.html

Check out this Web site for a lot of information on creatures of the prehistoric world. Don't miss the great pictures!

Winged Lizards
http://www.enchantedlearn-ing.com/subjects/dinosaurs/dinos/Pterosaur.shtml

Visit this Web site to learn all about the ancient world of flying reptiles.

Important Words

atmosphere the blanket of gases that surrounds Earth

brain cavity the opening in the skull where an animal's brain is located

crest a comb or a feathery tuft on the top of a creature's head

fossils evidence of plants and animals that lived long ago. Fossils might include bones, footprints, teeth, or leaf imprints on rocks.

predators animals that hunt other animals for food

prehistoric from the time before history was recorded

prey animals that are hunted by other animals for food

reptiles cold-blooded animals that usually crawl on the ground or creep on short legs

Index

Meet the Author

Award-winning author Elaine Landau worked as a newspaper reporter, an editor, and a youth-services librarian before becoming a full-time writer. She has written more than 250 nonfiction books for young people, including True Books on animals, countries, and food. Ms. Landau has a bachelor's degree in English and journalism from New York University as well as a master's degree in library and information science. She lives with her husband and son in Miami, Florida.